Contents

Welcome to football

Professional football is the most popular spectator sport in the world, watched either live at a match or on television by hundreds of millions of fans. Generally, fans share their passion between their national football team and a club team.

Every four years, national teams from around the world compete for the biggest prize in football: the **World Cup**. Representing your country in the World Cup is the highest honour a player can achieve. Winning it turns club stars into national legends.

Brazil has won the **World Cup** more times than any other country. It is also the only country to have qualified for all 20 tournaments (see pages 8–9).

Sándor Puhl, a top international referee, failed to show even a yellow card to an Italian player who elbowed a Spanish midfielder, and broke his nose, in the 1994 World Cup quarter-final between Italy and Spain. Italy won the match 2–1 and Spanish fans have blamed Puhl ever since (see pages 54–55).

The USA holds the record for lifting the **Women's World Cup** the most times – three! Germany have won it twice, and Japan and Norway once (see pages 12–13).

Only two World Cup finals have gone to **penalty shoot-outs**. Once was the 2006 final between Italy and France. Italy won 5–3. (see pages 50–51).

In 2006, Arsenal produced the **best defensive effort in the history** of the Champions League, going 10 games without conceding a goal (see pages 28–29).

In recent years, **club tournaments** like the Champions League, where clubs battle to be the top team in Europe, have become almost as popular as the World Cup. Clubs like Real Madrid, Barcelona and Manchester United are famous around the world.

The **Africa Cup of Nations** was first seen on television in Sudan in 1970. It is now televised around the world (see pages 18–19).

The first Premier League match took place in August 1992, with the first Premiership hat trick scored in the same month by Leeds' striker, Eric Cantona (see pages 20–21).

Even if you don't support the team, impressive midfielders, defenders, goal scorers and goalkeepers can be admired for their style and personality, on and off the pitch. Players like Maradona, Zoff and Cruyff are legends across the globe, inspiring fans with their talent and skill.

Brazil's Roberto Carlos was not just one of the **best left backs** in history, but one of the greatest free-kick takers too. Nicknamed 'the bullet man'. (see pages 45–46)

Danish goalkeeper **Peter Schmeichel** won the Danish Player of the Year award three times (see pages 46-47).

Pelé scored a record-breaking **1,281 goals** during his career (see pages 40–41).

History of football

The game of football, as we know it, has written rules, organisations and technology, but this is very different to the sport first invented. It all began with masses of people kicking a 'ball' across a rough piece of ground. It took years for the game to develop into today's massive spectator sport.

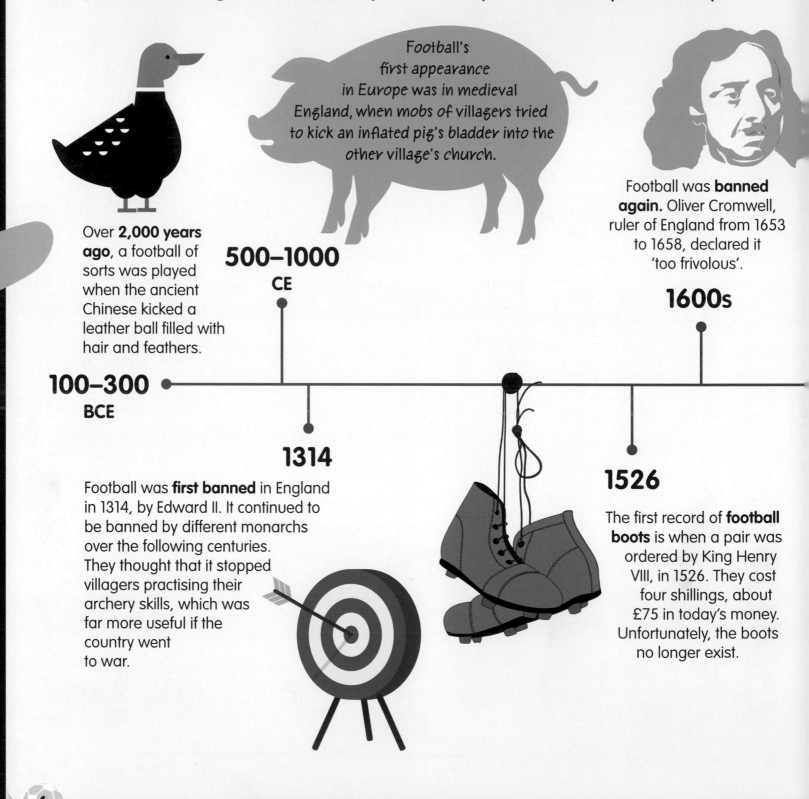

Football's first appearance in Europe was in medieval England, when mobs of villagers tried to kick an inflated pig's bladder into the other village's church.

Over **2,000 years ago**, a football of sorts was played when the ancient Chinese kicked a leather ball filled with hair and feathers.

500–1000
CE

Football was **banned again.** Oliver Cromwell, ruler of England from 1653 to 1658, declared it 'too frivolous'.

1600s

100–300
BCE

1314

Football was **first banned** in England in 1314, by Edward II. It continued to be banned by different monarchs over the following centuries. They thought that it stopped villagers practising their archery skills, which was far more useful if the country went to war.

1526

The first record of **football boots** is when a pair was ordered by King Henry VIII, in 1526. They cost four shillings, about £75 in today's money. Unfortunately, the boots no longer exist.

1872

The world's first-ever official **international match** took place between Scotland and England, in 1872 in Partick, Scotland. It was a 0–0 draw.

An English solicitor, Ebenezer Cobb Morley, is often thought of as the **father of modern football** because he set up its first governing body – the Football Association (FA) – in 1863. Morley also made an official list of rules, known as the Laws of the Game. These Laws are still being followed today and cover everything from the length of the match to penalties.

By 1900, Argentina, Italy, Germany and several other countries had all followed England in creating national governing bodies for football. The first international governing body (FIFA) was formed in 1904.

1863

1904

1891

Crossbars were first added to goal posts in the 1860s, and in 1891 a net was added to the goal.

1848

A set of **rules for football** was first drawn up in 1848 at Cambridge University, England. Although many early clubs developed their own rules – often just before each match started! The very first English football club, Sheffield FC, introduced the rules of free kicks, offside and half-time breaks.

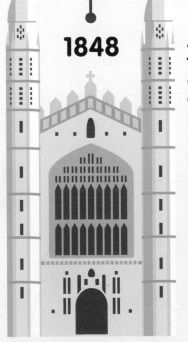

World Cup*

The FIFA World Cup is football's most important competition and the finals take place every four years. It is a knock-out tournament for the world's top 32 footballing nations. These teams are selected by qualifying competitions that involve countries from every corner of Earth. So, win the World Cup and you are truly the best footballing nation on the planet!

* Facts are correct up to and including the 2014 FIFA World Cup.

NO.1

The World Cup competition is the **most-watched sporting event** in the world.

Brazil is the only team to have played in every World Cup. They have also won the tournament more times than any other country.

Brazil	5
Italy	4
Germany	4
Argentina	2
Uruguay	2
France	1
Spain	1
England	1

MORE THAN **200** countries, from six continents compete in the World Cup, with 32 of these qualifying for the Finals. From 2026, the number of teams taking part in the World Cup Finals will increase to 48.

3.3 MILLION tickets were sold for the 2014 tournament in Brazil.

Two World Cup finals went to **penalty shoot-outs,** both involved Italy. They lost their shoot-out 3–2 to Brazil, in 1994, but won in 2006 against France, 5–3.

The **first World Cup** tournament took place in 1930. It was held in Uruguay.

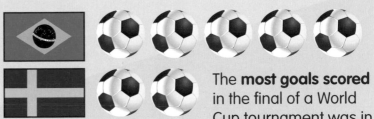

The **most goals scored** in the final of a World Cup tournament was in 1958, when Brazil beat Sweden 5–2.

FIFA

The international tournament is organised by the **Fédération Internationale de Football Association (FIFA).** It was originally founded in 1904 to organise a competition among eight European countries. It now has over 200 international associates from around the world.

An estimated **715 MILLION** people watched the **2014** tournament on television. That's an amazing **10 PER CENT** of the world's entire population!

The **highest-ever score** in a World Cup tournament was Austria 7–5 Switzerland in a quarter-final, in 1954.

Famous national teams: Brazil and Germany

These are two of the most successful national football teams ever. Between them, Brazil and Germany have lifted the World Cup trophy nine times. Both countries have produced some of the best players of all time.

Brazil won its third World Cup in 1970, with what is thought to be the greatest squad of players of all time. The team included Pelé, Jairzinho and Carlos Alberto Torres.

Brazilians are so fanatical about their national team that they stop working whenever Brazil play their World Cup matches. Shops and banks also close early.

Football is more than just a sport in Brazil – it is part of its culture. It is played everywhere, from the streets to the beaches, and is watched by just about everyone: men and women, young and old!

Brazil is the most successful country in the World Cup. It has qualified for all **20 World Cup** tournaments, and won it five times.

Brazilian football is known for its attractive style and flair. It has produced many of the world's best dribblers and free-kick takers.

BRAZIL vs GERMANY MATCHES

WINS 12
LOSSES 5
DRAWS 5

HALL OF FAME

BRAZIL

Pelé
considered a footballing legend all over the world

Garrincha
one of football's greatest dribblers

Didi
brilliant free-kick taker

Carlos Alberto Torres
one of the finest-ever defenders

Ronaldo Luís Nazário de Lima
played in three World Cups

Both countries have star players who have scored lots of goals and helped their country with the World Cup.

Ronald Luís Nazário de Lima scored **15 GOALS**

Miroslav Klose scored **16 GOALS**

Unlike many countries, in Germany there is much more fanatical support for the national team than for club teams. Up to a million Germans will gather in public places to watch World Cup games on giant screens.

German football is famed for its organisation and clinical goal scoring. They have also proved experts at penalty shoot-outs.

HALL OF FAME

GERMANY

Franz Beckenbauer
terrific German captain, then manager

Gerd Müller
scored 10 goals in 1970 World Cup

Karl-Heinz Rummenigge
high-scoring German winger

Lothar Matthäus
played in five World Cups

Sepp Maier
one of the greatest-ever goalkeepers.

Germany has produced three of the World Cup's **top six goal scorers:** Miroslav Klose, Gerd Müller and Jurgen Klinsmann.

7-1

This huge victory in the 2014 semi-final was Germany's best-ever performance in the World Cup. The unfortunate opponents were none other than Brazil!

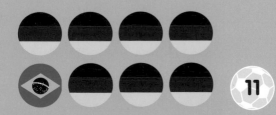

Women's World Cup*

Like the men's World Cup, the Women's World Cup is a tournament that takes place every four years, with qualifying matches happening beforehand. Even though the Women's World Cup only started in 1991, it has quickly grown in size and popularity.

* Facts are correct up to and including the 2015 FIFA Women's World Cup.

THE GREATEST PLAYERS AT THE WOMEN'S WORLD CUP

Brazil's Marta top scorer with 15 goals.

USA's Kristine Lilly played in an incredible five World Cups.

Germany's Birgit Prinz won two World Cups.

As a sign of the popularity of the Women's World Cup, over **90,000** TICKETS were sold for the **1999** final in California. This was a world record for a women's sporting event. The match was between the USA and China, the USA winning **5–4** after a penalty shoot-out.

Abby Wambach is the most successful **international goal** scorer in football history – for both men and women. She holds the record with 184 goals scored in international matches!

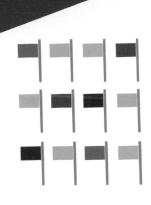

When the Women's World Cup started in **1991,** only **12** nations competed in the tournament. But by the time of the seventh World Cup in 2015, this number had **DOUBLED**, with teams from Europe, America, Africa and Asia competing.

The USA holds the record for lifting the Women's World Cup the most times: three. Germany have won it twice, and Japan and Norway once.

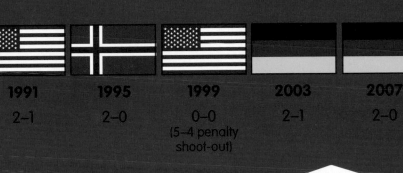

1991	1995	1999	2003	2007	2011	2015
2–1	2–0	0–0	2–1	2–0	2–2	5–2
		(5–4 penalty shoot-out)			(3–1 penalty shoot-out)	

The highest goal-scorer in a single Women's World Cup match is the USA's Michelle Akers. She scored **five goals** in a quarter-final game between the USA and Chinese Taipei, in 1991. USA went on to win the match 7–0!

1991

is when the first women's HAT TRICK was scored at the World Cup. The Italian striker Carolina Morace put three balls in the net against Chinese Taipei, securing the group match stages.

GOAL

Just as in the men's World Cup, **goal-line technology** (see pages 60–61) is now used in the women's tournaments to decide whether the ball fully crossed the line or not.

UEFA European Championship*

More commonly known as the Euros, the UEFA European Championship takes place every four years, midway between the World Cup finals. It is a knock-out tournament to decide which national team in Europe is the best. The 24 countries competing take it just as seriously as the World Cup itself.

* Facts are correct up to and including the 2016 UEFA European Championship.

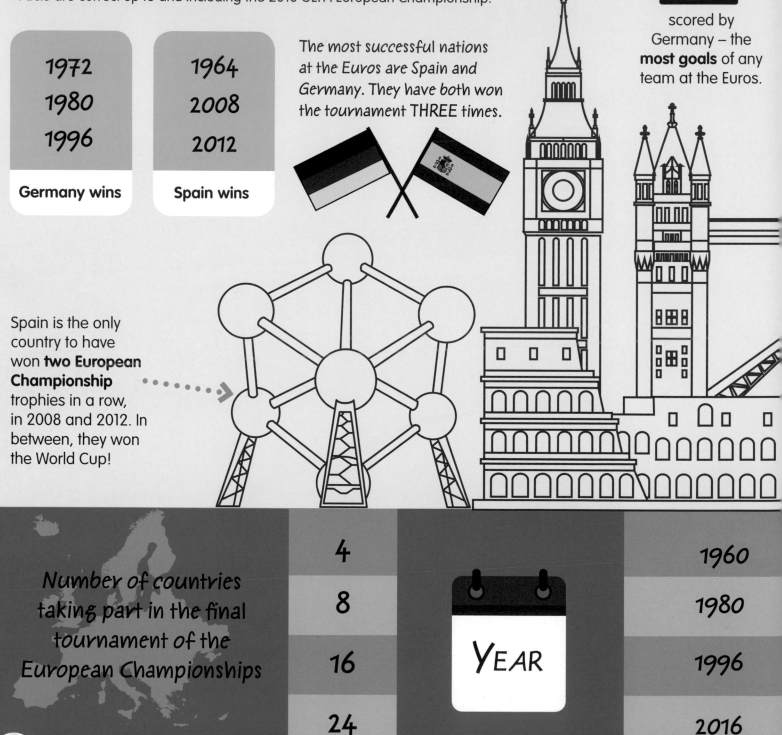

72 GOALS scored by Germany – the **most goals** of any team at the Euros.

1972 1980 1996	1964 2008 2012
Germany wins	**Spain wins**

The most successful nations at the Euros are Spain and Germany. They have both won the tournament THREE times.

Spain is the only country to have won **two European Championship** trophies in a row, in 2008 and 2012. In between, they won the World Cup!

Number of countries taking part in the final tournament of the European Championships		Year	
	4		1960
	8		1980
	16		1996
	24		2016

GERMANY HAS PLAYED THE MOST MATCHES AT THE EUROS, FOLLOWED BY THE NETHERLANDS, THEN SPAIN.

49	40	39
GERMANY	SPAIN	FRANCE

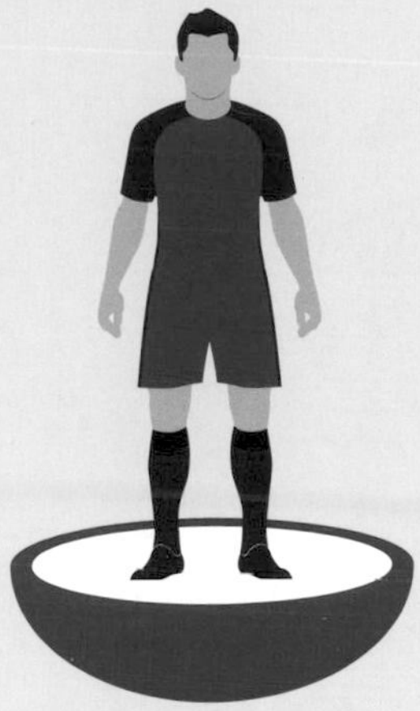

One of the greatest performers at the Euros, French midfielder Michel Platini, absolutely dominated the 1984 tournament. He scored a record NINE GOALS, including two hat tricks! Not bad for a midfielder.

The biggest shock at the Euros was in 2004, when minnows Greece beat host nation Portugal in the final 1–0.

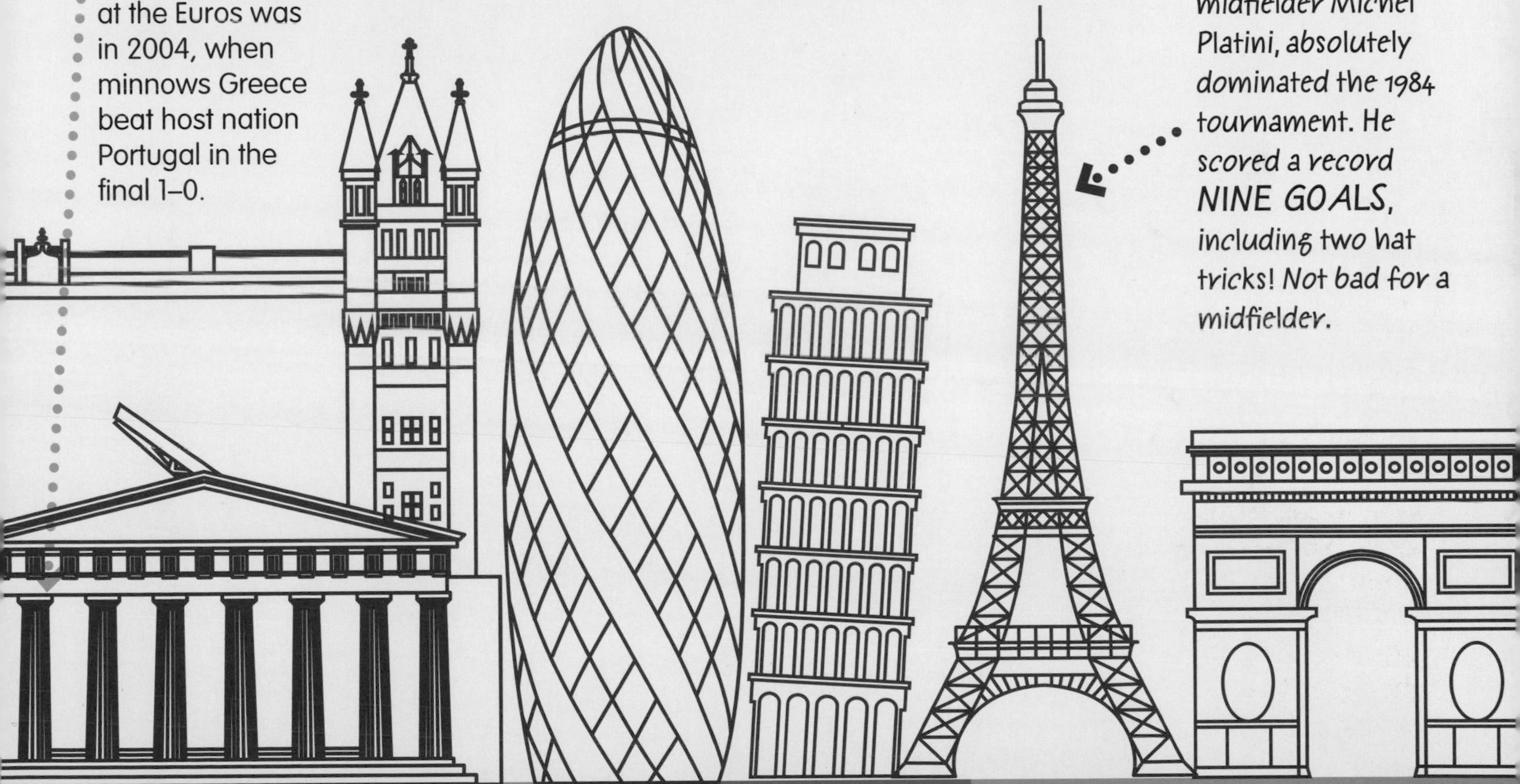

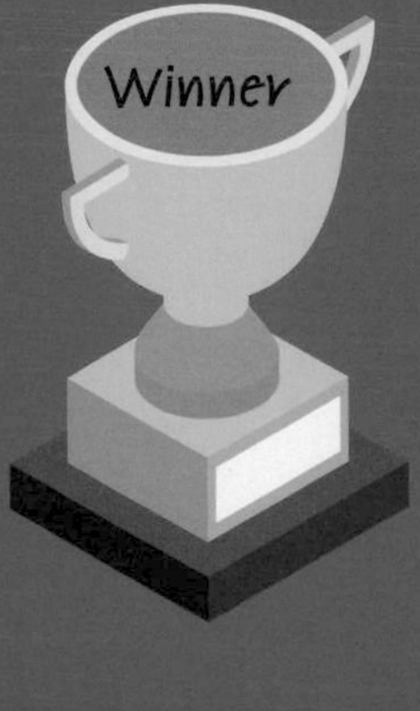

Host country	Winner
GERMANY	SOVIET UNION
ITALY	WEST GERMANY
ENGLAND	GERMANY
FRANCE	PORTUGAL

Copa América*

This is the South American version of the European Championship: a knock-out tournament to decide the top national football team. Twelve teams take part but only TEN play from South America. The other two teams are invited from outside of the continent. Mexico, the USA and Japan have all been guest teams.

* Facts are correct up to and including the 2016 Copa América.

Unlike most other international football tournaments, the Copa América isn't held regularly. Sometimes there's just one year between tournaments, and sometimes EIGHT!

In **1959**, there were two Copa América tournaments in just ONE YEAR! Argentina won the first and Uruguay the second.

Ecuador and Venezuela are the only South American teams never to have won the Copa América. Neither have any of the guest countries!

The Copa América is unusual in that **two trophies** are awarded at the end of the tournament. The Copa América trophy is awarded to the winner and the Copa Bolivia trophy to the runner-up.

15 URUGUAY   **14 ARGENTINA**

Uruguay is the most successful team at the Copa América, winning it **15 times**. But Argentina is close behind, with **14 wins**.

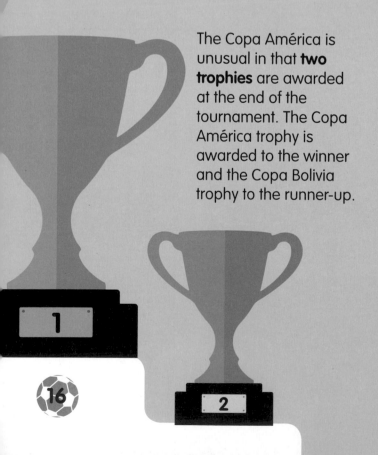

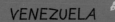

VENEZUELA

COLOMBIA

CUADOR

PERU

BRAZIL

Brazil's Pelé won **'best scorer'** in the first of the two 1959 tournaments, when he was just 18 years old. But Brazil lost the final to Argentina.

BOLIVIA

10
TEAMS

Messi was so disappointed that Argentina lost the 2015 final to Chile that he wouldn't accept his award for the tournament's best player.

PARAGUAY

The 2016 tournament celebrated the 100th anniversary of the Copa America. It was held in the USA, and 16 countries took part.

URUGUAY

ARGENTINA

Copa América matches tend to be very attack-minded, with an average of more than three goals per game.

CHILE

In the **1949** Copa América tournament, Brazil scored an amazing **43 GOALS** in just **SIX** matches. They scored **SEVEN GOALS** in the final!

The Africa Cup of Nations*

Africa's tournament to find the top footballing country in the continent is the Africa Cup of Nations. It is held every two years. The tournament is becoming more and more well known, and African players from top clubs are taking part.

* Facts are correct up to and including the 2017 Africa Cup of Nations.

The **coin toss** has played an important part in the winners' success at the Africa Cup of Nations.

In **1965**, Tunisia reached the final via a coin toss with Senegal.

A coin toss was used in **1988**, and helped Algeria reach the semi-finals against Ivory Coast.

The African Cup of Nations was first seen on television in Sudan, in 1970. It is now televised around the world.

Since the Africa Cup started in 1957, there have been THREE different trophies.

The original trophy was made of SILVER but Ghana was allowed to keep it after winning the tournament for the third time.

Cameroon also won the tournament three times and so they kept the second trophy.

The third trophy, plated in GOLD, was first awarded in 2002 and will be used until the next country has won three times.

TOP AFRICA CUP OF NATIONS GOAL-SCORERS:

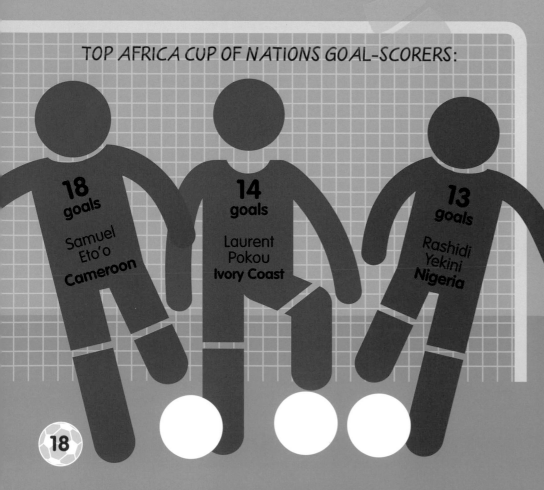

18 goals
Samuel Eto'o
Cameroon

14 goals
Laurent Pokou
Ivory Coast

13 goals
Rashidi Yekini
Nigeria

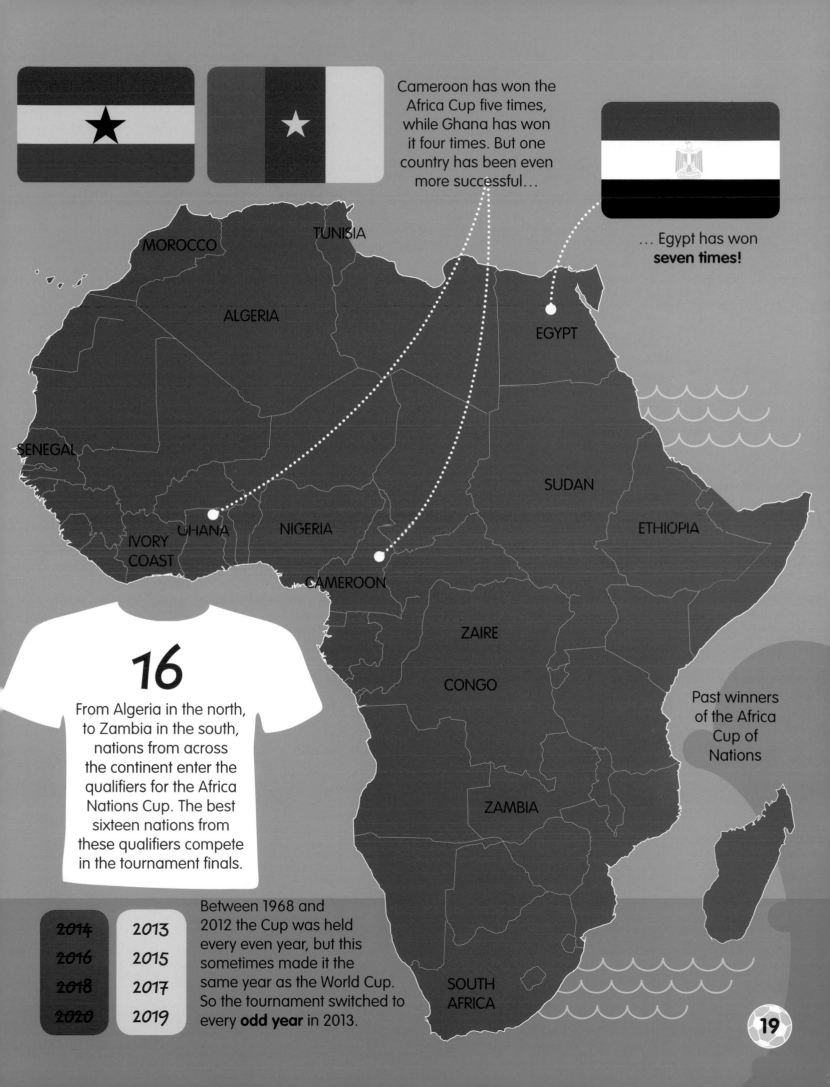

Cameroon has won the Africa Cup five times, while Ghana has won it four times. But one country has been even more successful…

… Egypt has won **seven times!**

MOROCCO

TUNISIA

ALGERIA

SENEGAL

EGYPT

SUDAN

GHANA

IVORY COAST

NIGERIA

ETHIOPIA

CAMEROON

ZAIRE

CONGO

Past winners of the Africa Cup of Nations

ZAMBIA

16

From Algeria in the north, to Zambia in the south, nations from across the continent enter the qualifiers for the Africa Nations Cup. The best sixteen nations from these qualifiers compete in the tournament finals.

SOUTH AFRICA

2014   2013
2016   2015
2018   2017
2020   2019

Between 1968 and 2012 the Cup was held every even year, but this sometimes made it the same year as the World Cup. So the tournament switched to every **odd year** in 2013.

English Premier League*

The Premier League consists of England's top 20 football clubs. During the football season, each team plays each other twice, once at home and once away. The team with the most points from all of these matches becomes the Premier League champion. The three teams with the least points are relegated to the league below.

* Facts are correct up to and including the 2016 English Premier League.

The first Premier League match took place in **August 1992**. The first Premier League hat trick was scored in the same month by Leeds' striker Eric Cantona.

Moving to Manchester United, Cantona became the Premier League's earliest big star and helped his team to win a string of titles.

The Premier League's **highest goal-scorer** is Alan Shearer with 260 goals.

The **most successful** manager is Sir Alex Ferguson who led Manchester United to win a staggering 13 titles.

The **highest attendance** at a Premier League match was over 76,000 for the Manchester United versus Blackburn game, in March 2007.

Manchester United's Ryan Giggs played the **most seasons** in the Premier League: from its launch in 1992 to his retirement in 2014.

The **most surprising** Premier League win was Leicester City in 2016. The odds of them achieving this were very small at the beginning of the season – just 5,000/1.

Chelsea have the **worst disciplinary record** with over 1,200 bookings.

During the 2015 season, more than **13 MILLION** fans attended Premier League games. Over **950,000** fans came from overseas.

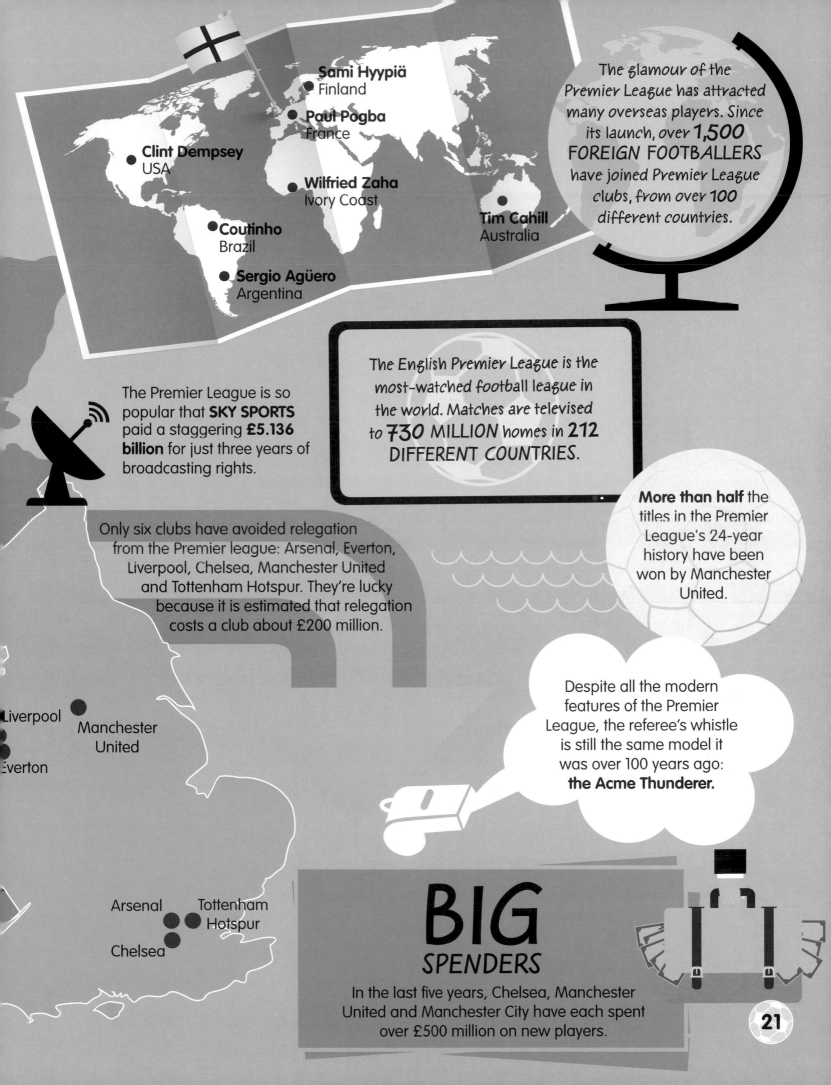

Sami Hyypiä
Finland

Paul Pogba
France

Clint Dempsey
USA

Wilfried Zaha
Ivory Coast

Coutinho
Brazil

Tim Cahill
Australia

Sergio Agüero
Argentina

The glamour of the Premier League has attracted many overseas players. Since its launch, over **1,500 FOREIGN FOOTBALLERS** have joined Premier League clubs, from over **100** different countries.

The Premier League is so popular that **SKY SPORTS** paid a staggering **£5.136 billion** for just three years of broadcasting rights.

The English Premier League is the most-watched football league in the world. Matches are televised to **730 MILLION** homes in **212 DIFFERENT COUNTRIES.**

More than half the titles in the Premier League's 24-year history have been won by Manchester United.

Only six clubs have avoided relegation from the Premier league: Arsenal, Everton, Liverpool, Chelsea, Manchester United and Tottenham Hotspur. They're lucky because it is estimated that relegation costs a club about £200 million.

Despite all the modern features of the Premier League, the referee's whistle is still the same model it was over 100 years ago: **the Acme Thunderer.**

Liverpool

Manchester United

Everton

Arsenal   Tottenham Hotspur

Chelsea

BIG
SPENDERS

In the last five years, Chelsea, Manchester United and Manchester City have each spent over £500 million on new players.

Serie A*

Serie A is the top Italian league and it's thought of as one of the best tournaments on the planet. Competing in Serie A are three of the world's most famous clubs: Juventus, AC Milan and Inter Milan.

* Facts are correct up to and including the 2016 Serie A.

THE TEAMS WITH THE MOST SERIE A WINS ARE:

31 JUVENTUS

18 AC MILAN

18 INTER MILAN

3 ROMA

2 LAZIO

THE ITALIAN CUP

1

Alongside the Serie A league is Italy's knock-out tournament, the Coppa Italia. Juventus hold the **record for winning** this the most times: 11.

THE OLD LADY

is the nickname for Juventus, one of the most successful and best-supported clubs in the world. Juventus have twice gone on to win the Champions League, which decides the top team in Europe.

Inter Milan were one of the very first teams to include players from abroad. They took on a foreign player, **Hernst Marktl** from Switzerland, in 1908 and made him the team's captain.

Like Roma, Lazio are **based in Rome**. Despite sharing the same ground for many years, there is fierce rivalry between the two clubs.

Silvio Piola is the highest goal scorer in Serie A's history, netting 274 goals in his 25-year career.

The Serie A **record transfer** was paid for Gonzalo Higuaín in 2016. He moved from Napoli to Juventus for €90 MILLION.

The **biggest stadium** is San Siro. It is shared by AC Milan and Inter Milan.

Paolo Maldini played in the **most matches** in Serie A. He appeared in 647 matches, all for AC Milan, between 1984–2009.

Inter Milan hold the record for **most seasons** in Serie A: 7.

The **oldest player** in Serie A was Marco Ballotta at 44 years, 38 days. Amedeo Amadei, who was only 15 years, 280 days when he first played for AS Roma was the **youngest**.

MOST GOALS

274

The longest **UNBEATEN** streak in Serie A belongs to AC Milan. They won or drew a massive **58 GAMES** in a row, from 1991–1993.

AC Milan · Fiorentina · Inter · Juventus · Roma · Lazio · SSC Napoli

SEVEN SISTERS

These clubs are known as the Seven Sisters of Italian football. They have qualified in the top seven positions in most Serie A seasons. SSC Napoli has replaced Parma in recent years.

The Serie A league is often called the **Scudetto** – 'small shield'. This is because the winning team is allowed to wear a small shield on their shirts for the following season.

La Liga*

Spain's top league, La Liga, is made up of the country's best 20 clubs. It has attracted some of the best foreign footballers of all time, including Diego Maradona, Lionel Messi and Cristiano Ronaldo.

* Facts are correct up to and including the 2016 La Liga.

LA LIGA'S HIGHEST GOAL-SCORERS ARE:

#	Player	Nationality		Goals
1	Lionel Messi	Argentinian		337 goals
2	Cristiano Ronaldo	Portuguese		272 goals
3	Telmo Zarra	Spanish		251 goals
4	Hugo Sánchez	Mexican		234 goals
5	Raúl González Blanco	Spanish		228 goals

Spanish and foreign players competing in La Liga have repeatedly won the **world's top footballer** awards.

11
World Player of the Year

19
Ballon d'Or
A yearly award given by FIFA and *France Football*.

4
Best Player in Europe

Many regard Barcelona's world-class attacking trio of Messi, Neymar and Suárez as the greatest striking force of all time.

Since La Liga's launch in 1929, **60 different clubs** have taken one of its 20 places.

Clubs playing in La Liga have won more Champions League titles than clubs from any other European league.

La Liga clubs have won **16** of the Champions League tournaments, with Real Madrid winning a record **11** of these.

La Liga's two **most famous grounds** are Real Madrid's Bernabéu, which holds more than **80,000 fans**, and Barcelona's Nou Camp, which seats **nearly 100,000** people.

La Liga side Espanyol are known as the **'perriquitos'** – the budgies. This is because they originally played on a pitch surrounded by palm trees full of the colourful birds.

NINE different teams have been crowned La Liga champions since the tournament began in **1928**. Real Madrid have won a record **32** times. Their fierce rival, Barcelona, have won it **24** times.

32	24	10	8	6	2	1	1	1

Real Madrid	Barcelona	Atlético Madrid	Athletic Bilbao	Valencia	Real Sociedad	Real Betis	Sevilla	Deportivo La Coruña

Bundesliga*

The 18-team Bundesliga is Germany's top league. Each team plays each other twice, once at home and once away. The team with the most points from the matches becomes Bundesliga champion. Unlike many other European premier leagues, the Bundesliga teams 'home grow' lots of their players, promoting them from their academies.

* Facts are correct up to and including the 2016 League.

Hamburg SV

Schalke 04

Borussia Dortmund

Four Bundesliga clubs are among the world's **MOST VALUABLE** football clubs:

The Bundesliga is one of the world's **most popular leagues**, with matches broadcast to over 200 countries. Television pays over **€1 billion** per year for screening rights.

Since the Bundesliga's launch in **1962**, a total of **53** German clubs have taken one of its **18** places.

During each season, fans at Bundesliga matches make their way through a massive amount of refreshment. Spectators at the huge Allianz Arena, shared by Bayern Munich and 1860 Munich, munched nearly **25,000 SAUSAGES!**

The Bundesliga is Europe's second most successful league, only behind Spain's La Liga, based on performances in the Champions League and Europa League.

The average attendance for a Bundesliga match is over

45,000

That's more fans per match than any other football league IN THE WORLD!

👤 = 1,000

Bayern Munich

26

Bayern Munich is the **most successful team** in German football history, winning the Bundesliga a record **26 times**, and Germany's knock-out cup more times than anyone else. They are also the only German club to have won all the major European competitions.

All-time great players in the Bundesliga over the years include Bayern Munich's **Franz Beckenbauer**, **Gerd Müller** and **Miroslave Klose**, and Hamburg SV's **Uwe Seeler**.

Champions League*

The Champions League is a yearly competition between the best clubs in Europe. To qualify for the competition, a club must have come top, or near the top in the previous season of their country's top league.

* Facts are correct up to and including the 2016 Champions League.

An estimated 360 million viewers watch the final of the Champions League, making it the **most watched annual sporting event** on the planet.

The Champions League begins in MID-JULY and runs through to the packed and atmospheric final in MAY, in following year.

January	February	March	April
May	June	July	August
September	October	November	December

FINAL

KNOCK-OUT ROUNDS

Last 16

Quarter-final

Semi-final

Final

WINNER

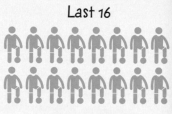

2

1

3

4

The Champions League started in 1992. It was preceded by the European Cup, with only the **top team** from each national league taking part. But the Champions League allows nations to enter their next best teams as well. The bigger football nations like Spain, Italy and England can enter their **four best teams** into the competition.

28

The most successful club in the Champions League history is Spain's Real Madrid, winning **11 TIMES**.

Real Madrid ⭐⭐⭐⭐⭐⭐⭐⭐⭐⭐⭐

AC Milan ⭐⭐⭐⭐⭐⭐⭐

Bayern Munich ⭐⭐⭐⭐⭐

Barcelona ⭐⭐⭐⭐⭐

Liverpool ⭐⭐⭐⭐⭐

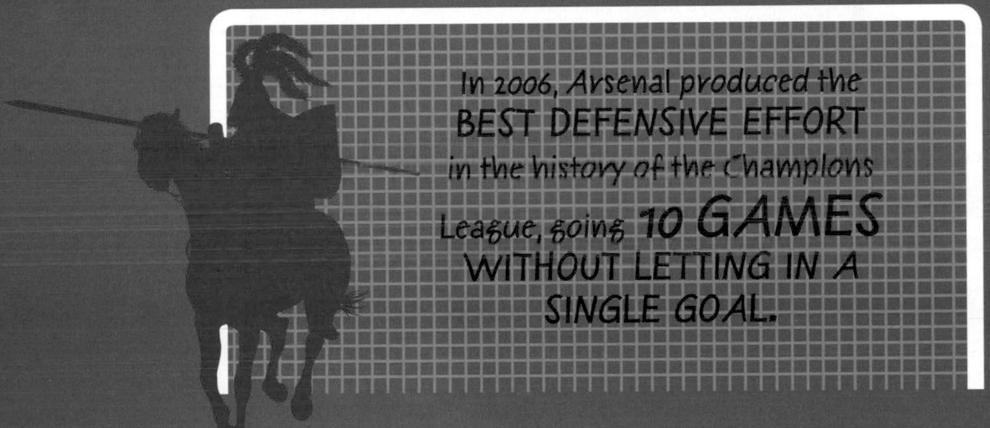

The group stage kicks off the Champions League, with every team in each group playing everyone else. The top two from each group then go through to four knock-out rounds: the 'last 16', quarter-final, semi-final and then the final.

In 2006, Arsenal produced the **BEST DEFENSIVE EFFORT** in the history of the Champions League, going **10 GAMES** WITHOUT LETTING IN A SINGLE GOAL.

PRIZE MONEY
Quarter-finals: **€6 MILLION**

Semi-finals: **€7 MILLION**

Runner-up: **€10.5 MILLION**

Winner: **€15 MILLION**

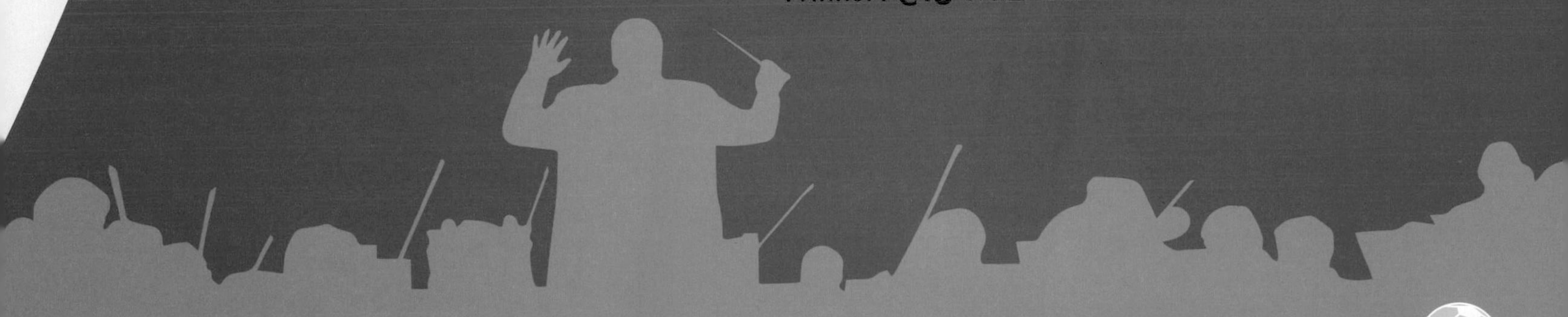

The Champions League's rousing anthem, written by Englishman Tony Britten, is played at Champions League matches and is a popular tune on television.

Copa Libertadores*

The South American equivalent of the Champions League is the Copa Libertadores. It is so popular that it has become part of South American culture. Many South American players say they would rather play in the Copa Libertadores than make big-money moves to European clubs.

* Facts are correct up to and including the 2016 Copa Libertadores.

MOST WINS

7	INDEPENDIENTE	ARGENTINA
6	BOCA JUNIORS	ARGENTINA
5	PEÑAROL	URUGUAY

BRAZILIAN CLUBS

ARGENTINIAN CLUBS

The **most successful** teams in the Copa Libertadores are clubs from Argentina, who have won 24 times, and clubs from Brazil, who have won 17 times.

17

24

An average of **80,000 SPECTATORS** watch the two-legged final of the Copa Libertadores, which is televised to more than **135 COUNTRIES** around the globe.

👤 = 4,000

South American clubs invest **MILLIONS** in top-price players to give them a chance of winning the title.

11	2
PEÑAROL	VALENCIA

The **biggest victory** in the Copa Libertadores was in 1970 when Uruguayan club Peñarol beat Venezuelan club Valencia.

The intercontinental Cup, begun in 1960, was a two-legged annual competition between the winners of the Copa Libertadores and the European Champions League. It pitched the best team in Europe against the best team in South America. However, the matches were often very violent, with players sometimes left with broken noses! In 1980, the Intercontinental Cup was replaced by the Toyota Cup but many of the problems continued and so the idea was eventually abandoned.

The top scorer in the Copa Libertadores is Alberto Spencer from Uruguayan club Peñarol. He scored **54 GOALS**. That is **17** more than the second top scorer, Fernando Morena.

The **FASTEST GOAL** during the Copa Libertadores was scored in **1976** by Félix Suárez for Alianza Lima. It was just **SIX SECONDS** into the game!

The winner of the Copa Libertadores qualifies for the **Club World Cup.** This is an annual knock-out competition to find the best club team in the world and involves the top clubs from all the world's continents.

FA Cup*

The English FA Cup is the most famous national knock-out competition in the world. Premier League giants and small amateur teams can all enter, which makes it such an exciting tournament. A random draw for each round could pitch your tiny local club against a super club. Very occasionally, the tiny club wins!

* Facts are correct up to and including the 2016 FA Cup.

MOST CUP WINS OF ALL TIME:

MANCHESTER CITY	5
EVERTON	5
BLACKBURN ROVERS	6
NEWCASTLE UNITED	6
LIVERPOOL	7
CHELSEA	7
ASTON VILLA	7
TOTTENHAM HOTSPUR	8
MANCHESTER UNITED	11
ARSENAL	12

Penalty shoot-outs are used i earlier rounds of the FA Cup if t tie is still drawn after a replay. later rounds, drawn ties do no go to a replay but are decided by penalty shoot-outs straightaway. The longest-ever penalty shoot-out in the FA Cup was in the replay tie between Tunbridge wells and Littlehampton Town. Tunbridge Wells won the shoot-out 16-15!

Ashley Cole is the **most decorated** FA Cup player. He has been on the winning team seven times: **three** with Arsenal in 2002, 2003 and 2005, and **four** with Chelsea in 2007, 2009, 2010 and 2012.

The idea for the FA Cup came from CW Alcock, the captain of a team called Wanderers. It was also Wanderers who were the first winners!

The FA Cup started in **1871**, making it the oldest footballing competition in the world.

THE CUP FINAL

is traditionally held at Wembley Stadium in London. Chelsea was the last team to win at the old Wembley Stadium and the first to win in the new Wembley Stadium, in **2007**.

More than **700 teams** take part in the FA Cup. There are 14 rounds, each a straight knock-out. Small amateur teams enter at the very first preliminary rounds in August, but the top league teams do not enter until January.

The extreme weather conditions in the winter of 1963, known as the **Big Freeze**, meant that most of the FA Cup's third-round matches had to be postponed. It took 66 days to complete them all!

The FA Cup has a history of small teams beating big clubs, and they're known as **Giant Killers**.

1964 – Oxford United **3**, Blackburn Rovers **1**

1971 – Colchester United **3**, Leeds United **2**

1980 – Harlow **1**, Leicester City **0**

1992 – Wrexham **2**, Arsenal **1**

2011 – Stevenage Borough **3**, Newcastle **1**

Shock Winners

1973
Sunderland
beat Leeds, 1–0

1976
Southampton beat
Manchester United, 1–0

1988
Wimbledon
beat Liverpool, 1–0

2013
Wigan beat
Manchester City, 1–0

First televised in **1938**, today the FA Cup final has an estimated TV audience of HALF A BILLION PEOPLE.

The **FA Cup trophy** is decorated with ribbons of both team's colours at the start of the final. But when the match has been won, the loser's ribbons are removed.

Mega-clubs: the biggest and richest

Professional football has become big business, with some of the richest clubs valued at more than £1 BILLION. Top clubs earn their money from selling match tickets, sponsorship deals, TV and satellite income, and the sale of club merchandise, such as replica shirts.

THE WORLD'S RICHEST clubs are all based in Europe, with Spanish and English clubs holding the top four places.

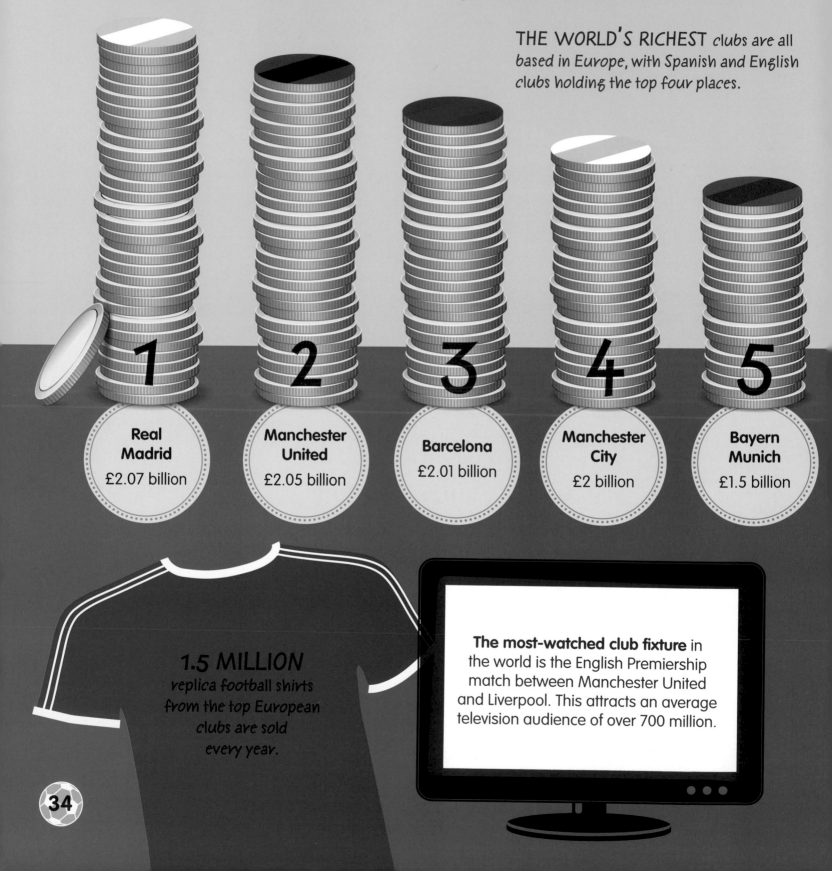

1

Real Madrid

£2.07 billion

2

Manchester United

£2.05 billion

3

Barcelona

£2.01 billion

4

Manchester City

£2 billion

5

Bayern Munich

£1.5 billion

1.5 MILLION replica football shirts from the top European clubs are sold every year.

The most-watched club fixture in the world is the English Premiership match between Manchester United and Liverpool. This attracts an average television audience of over 700 million.

PARIS SAINT-GERMAIN

★ ★ ★
SEASON TICKET
£3,600
That's how much Italian club AC Milan charges for a season ticket, making it the **most expensive in the world.**

Manchester United have nearly **30** DIFFERENT SPONSORS, ranging from airlines to sportswear companies. They pay the club nearly **€150 MILLION PER YEAR.**

6

7

8

9

10

Chelsea
£870 million

Arsenal
£832 million

Liverpool
£624 million

Juventus
£531 million

AC Milan
£492 million

Manchester United has the most expensive squad in the world, valued at over
£620 MILLION.
The club paid £150 million for just two players: £60 million for Angel Di Maria and £90 million for Paul Pogba.

Real Madrid's Cristiano Ronaldo earned a mind-boggling
£16.6 MILLION
in sponsorship in just one year.

Local rivals: famous derbies

A 'derby match' is one between two teams from the same city or town, or from cities that are very close to each other. Derbies are usually very passionate contests, both on and off the pitch, and fans often care more about winning a derby match than beating a team that would push them higher up the league table.

10 TOP EUROPEAN DERBIES

1 **Celtic vs Rangers** (Glasgow, Scotland)

2 **Galatasaray vs Fenerbahçe** (Istanbul, Turkey)

3 **Red Star Belgrade vs Partizan Belgrade** (Belgrade, Serbia)

4 **Roma vs Lazio** (Rome, Italy)

5 **Olympiacos vs Panathinaikos** (Athens, Greece)

6 **AC Milan vs Inter Milan** (Milan, Italy)

7 **Liverpool vs Everton** (Liverpool, England)

8 **Dinamo Bucureşti vs Steaua Bucureşti** (Bucharest, Romania)

9 **Sevilla vs Real Betis** (Seville, Spain)

10 **Tottenham Hotspur vs Arsenal** (London, England)

Derby games often reflect the **historical, cultural and religious backgrounds** of the two teams. Scottish clubs Celtic and Rangers both come from Glasgow, but Celtic has a strong Catholic base and Rangers a Protestant one.

One of the BIGGEST ENGLISH DERBIES is between LIVERPOOL AND EVERTON.
Their two grounds are separated only by a park, but that does nothing to reduce the intense rivalry between the two sets of fans.

Italy's biggest derbies are Roma against Lazio, who are both from Rome, and AC Milan against Inter Milan, both from Milan. The matches are full of boisterous atmosphere: with flares, horns and trumpets, making plenty of noise.

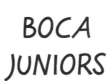

GALATASARAY VS FENERBAHÇE

This has always *been one of the most* VIOLENT *European derbies, with* FIREWORKS, BURNING FLAGS *and often* PUNCH–UPS. *Both clubs are based in the Turkish capital of Istanbul: Galatasaray are from the European side of the city and Fenerbahçe are from the Asian side of the city.*

BOCA JUNIORS VS RIVER PLATE

The most famous derby outside Europe is between **Argentinian clubs Boca juniors and River Plate**, both based in the capital Buenos Aires. Boca Juniors, from a poorer part of the city, are called 'little pigs' by opposing fans, while River Plate are accused of being 'chickens'.

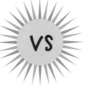

Stadiums

Just as football clubs vary in size, so do the football grounds the teams play at. Some stadiums are just as famous as big clubs and star players. They can seat thousands of people, create a special atmosphere and people even get married in them!

WEMBLEY FACTS

- The newly built Wembley Stadium was completed in 2007. More than **3,500** construction workers helped build it.

- It would take you about **15 MINUTES** to walk all the way round the stadium's **1 KILOMETRE** circumference.

- The stadium's arch is more than **1.5 TIMES HIGHER** than the STATUE OF LIBERTY.

- The stadium contains **2,618 TOILETS** – more than any other stadium in the world!

Manchester United's stadium, **Old Trafford**, is famous for the attractive style of football that has been played there over the years. Fans lovingly refer to it as the 'Theatre of Dreams'.

The **Estadio Azteca Stadium** in Mexico City, home of the Mexican national team, is one of the largest stadiums in the world, holding nearly 87,000 fans. It has hosted two World Cup tournaments.

EUROPE'S LARGEST FOOTBALL STADIUMS

Home to FC Barcelona, with a capacity of 99,786, the **Camp Nou** is the largest club-owned stadium on the planet.

Wembley Stadium	England	90,000
Signal Iduna Park	Germany	81,359
Bernabéu (Real Madrid)	Spain	81,044
San Siro (AC Milan/Inter Milan)	Italy	80,018

France's magnificent **STADE DE FRANCE** is home to the national side. It was built when France hosted the World Cup in **1998**, and also used for the Rugby World Cup in **2007**.

The **Luzhniki Stadium in Moscow, Russia** will host the final of the 2018 World Cup. It is one of the few top stadiums to have an artificial pitch, which is needed to cope with the extreme cold of Moscow winters.

2018

DRNOVICE STADIUM in the Czech Republic only has a capacity of **7,500.** even though the tiny town's entire population is just **2,300** – so that's **THREE** seats for every person!

The **Bernabéu** is home to Real Madrid and has played host to four Champions League finals and the 1982 World Cup final.

The San Siro is the home of both AC Milan and Inter Milan. It is the only stadium in the world to have been the regular home to two separate winners of the Champions League.

Goal-scorers

Who do fans consider the most exciting players on the pitch? The big goal-scorers, of course. These are the players that become football's biggest idols and demand the highest transfer fees. Many of the world's top strikers now move clubs for at least £50 million and become international superstars.

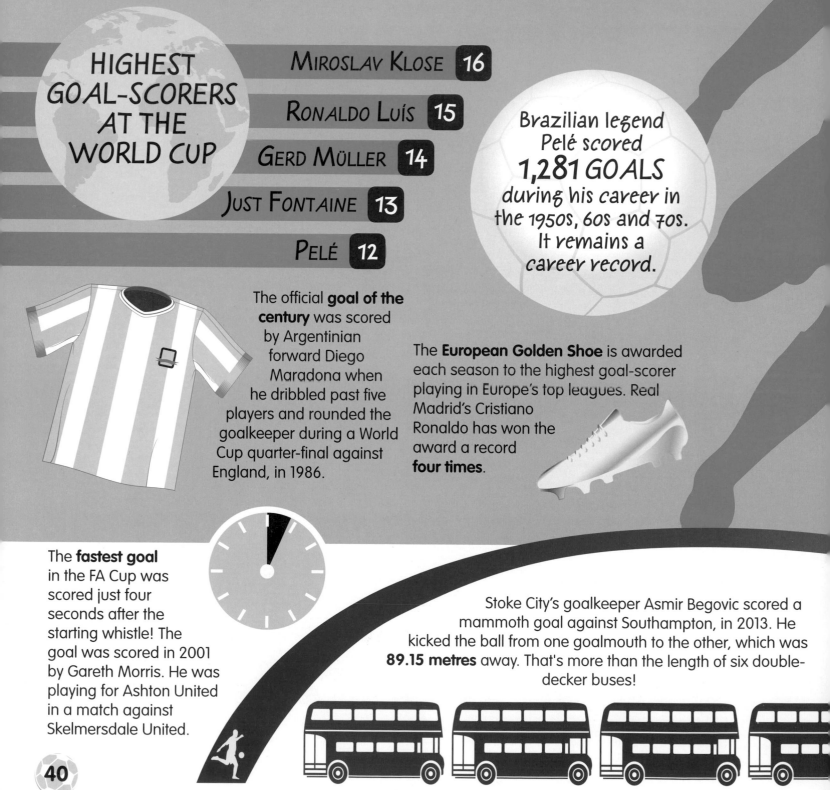

HIGHEST GOAL-SCORERS AT THE WORLD CUP

MIROSLAV KLOSE **16**

RONALDO LUÍS **15**

GERD MÜLLER **14**

JUST FONTAINE **13**

PELÉ **12**

Brazilian legend Pelé scored **1,281 GOALS** during his career in the 1950s, 60s and 70s. It remains a career record.

The official **goal of the century** was scored by Argentinian forward Diego Maradona when he dribbled past five players and rounded the goalkeeper during a World Cup quarter-final against England, in 1986.

The **European Golden Shoe** is awarded each season to the highest goal-scorer playing in Europe's top leagues. Real Madrid's Cristiano Ronaldo has won the award a record **four times**.

The **fastest goal** in the FA Cup was scored just four seconds after the starting whistle! The goal was scored in 2001 by Gareth Morris. He was playing for Ashton United in a match against Skelmersdale United.

Stoke City's goalkeeper Asmir Begovic scored a mammoth goal against Southampton, in 2013. He kicked the ball from one goalmouth to the other, which was **89.15 metres** away. That's more than the length of six double-decker buses!

The **most goals** scored (in the opposite teams' goal) in a single match was by Cypriot striker Panagiotis Pontikos. He scored 16 of the goals in his team's 24–3 win in a Cypriot third Division game, in 2007.

149 HOME **0** AWAY

The highest victory on record was in a **2002** match between two sides from Madagascar, AS Adena and SO L'Emyrne. But all **149 GOALS** were OWN GOALS, deliberately scored by SO L'Emyrne in protest at a refereeing decision.

Players who have scored 45 goals or more for their country:

Robbie Keane
IRELAND
68

Zlatan Ibrahimović
SWEDEN
62

Didier Drogba
IVORY COAST
65

David Villa
SPAIN
59

Samuel Eto'o
CAMEROON
56

Cristiano Ronaldo
PORTUGAL
68

Wayne Rooney
ENGLAND
53

Thierry Henry
FRANCE
51

Luis Suárez
URUGUAY
46

Lionel Messi
ARGENTINA
57

RICHARD DUNNE heads the English Premier League's top scorers list – but for goals at the wrong end! Dunne has scored a record **10** OWN GOALS.

Midfielders

Midfielders form the link between defenders and forwards. Some play a more defensive role and others a more attacking role. Others are known as 'box-to-box' midfielders, and have both roles. These are the players who tend to cover the most ground during a match, one moment deep in their own half and the next running fast into the opposition's.

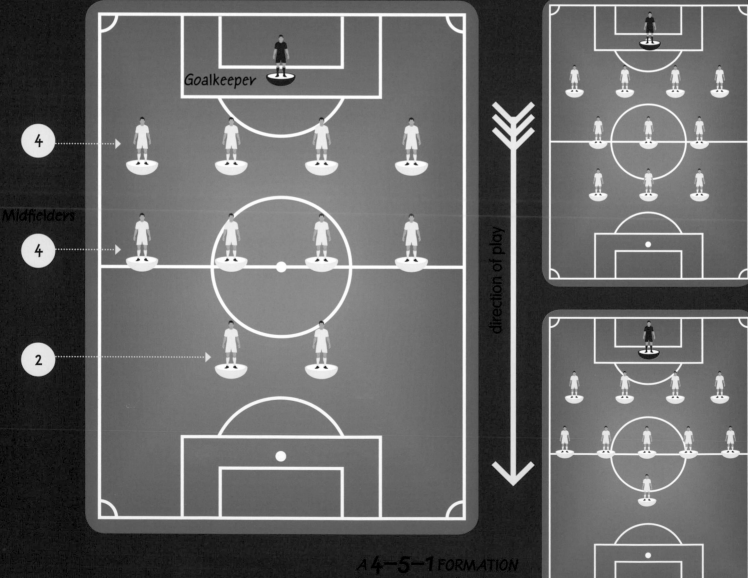

TEAM FORMATION is usually expressed as a series of numbers. For example, 4–4–2 means four players in defence, four in midfield and two up front.

A 4–3–3 FORMATION describes a light midfield.

Goalkeeper

4

Midfielders

4

2

direction of play

A 4–5–1 FORMATION 'swamps' the midfield.

The destroyers are the strong and uncompromising midfielders who play a more defensive role. Their job is to break up the other team's attack!

Right-footed midfielders normally play on the right wing and left-footed players on the left wing. However, some midfielders like to switch wings, sometimes even during the course of a match.

The creators are the more attacking midfielders. Their job is to 'assist' the strikers with clever passes and crosses.

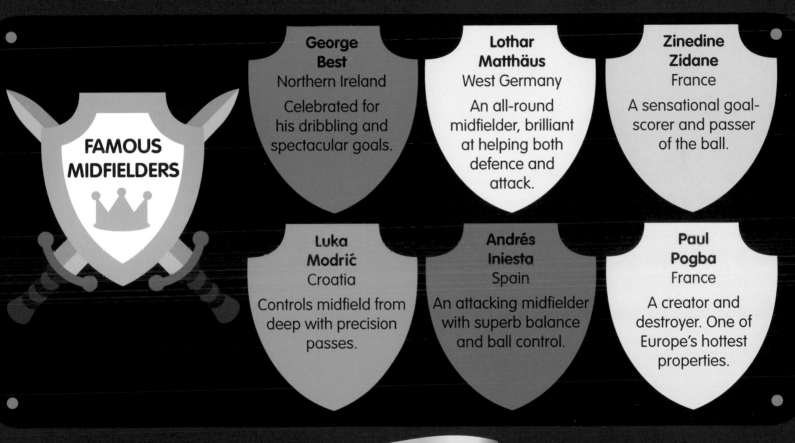

FAMOUS MIDFIELDERS

George Best
Northern Ireland
Celebrated for his dribbling and spectacular goals.

Lothar Matthäus
West Germany
An all-round midfielder, brilliant at helping both defence and attack.

Zinedine Zidane
France
A sensational goal-scorer and passer of the ball.

Luka Modrić
Croatia
Controls midfield from deep with precision passes.

Andrés Iniesta
Spain
An attacking midfielder with superb balance and ball control.

Paul Pogba
France
A creator and destroyer. One of Europe's hottest properties.

HALL OF FAME

Johan Cruyff
Netherlands
Decades active: 1960s–80s

Cruyff was a creative playmaker with a superb football brain. His dribbling, passing and vision created chance after chance for his strikers, and he scored many goals himself. The famous 'Cruyff turn', where he looked as though he was going to cross the ball but spun it round the defender instead, is part of footballing legend.

Diego Maradona
Argentina
Decades active: 1970s–90s

Perhaps the greatest dribbler of all time, Maradona was small and stocky and had superb control – the ball almost seemed to stick to his feet. The undisputed star of the 1986 World Cup, many regard Maradona as the most exciting player ever to put on a pair of football boots.

Defenders

The main responsibility of a defender is to stop their opponents from scoring. Some defenders are small and fast, skilled at taking the ball from the striker. Others are tall and agile; their job is to out-jump the strikers at crosses and corners. Modern defenders are often expected to play a role in attack as well.

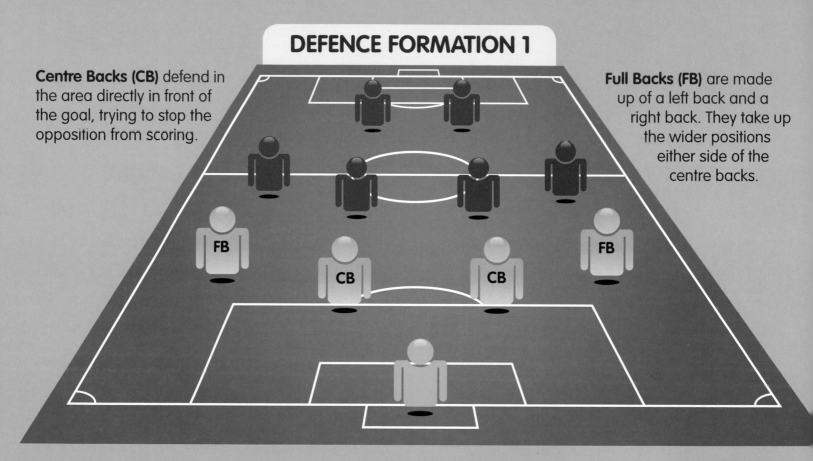

DEFENCE FORMATION 1

Centre Backs (CB) defend in the area directly in front of the goal, trying to stop the opposition from scoring.

Full Backs (FB) are made up of a left back and a right back. They take up the wider positions either side of the centre backs.

BRAZIL'S ROBERTO CARLOS was not just one of the best left backs in history, but one of the greatest free-kick takers too. Nicknamed 'THE BULLET MAN', Carlos' free kicks travelled at over **137** KILOMETRES PER HOUR and had a famous bend in the air.

Italy's Paolo Maldini is universally considered the greatest defender of recent times. His skill at adapting meant that he could play just about anywhere in defence: left back, right back or centre back. He was tough and intelligent, and even the world's greatest strikers feared him.

Franz Beckenbauer was the most skilful defender of all time. For many years the German captain refined the role of the 'sweeping' defender so defence could be switched quickly into attack. He would often race the length of the pitch to finish off the move he started by scoring the goal.

Bobby Moore was England's captain during their World Cup success of 1966. He's probably only behind Beckenbauer and Maldini as the finest defender ever. He was not fast, but read the game better than just about anyone, with perfectly timed tackles.

Some defenders are quite small, but they make up for their size with pace and technique. A perfect example is Germany's world-class defender Philipp Lahm, nicknamed the "Magic Dwarf".

TODAY'S BEST DEFENDERS

1	PHILIPP LAHM	Impeccable right back.
2	DIEGO GODÍN	World-class centre back.
3	DAVID ALABA	Versatile left back.
4	GIORGIO CHIELLINI	Commanding centre back.
5	RAPHAËL VARANE	Stylish centre back.

Sweeper (SW) is a third centre back, but with a much more fluid role. While the other centre backs have the very specific role of marking opponents, the sweeper moves around and behind the defence, "sweeping up" loose balls or players that find a way through.

DEFENCE FORMATION 2

WB CB SW CB WB

Wing Backs (WB) are the modern version of full backs. Their main job is to defend, but when the pressure is off, they are encouraged to race up the left or right wing to assist the attack.

45

GOAL HEIGHT
base to crossbar –
2.44 M (8 FT)

2.1 M

TALLEST KEEPER
Belgian Kristof Van Hout – **2.08 M**

1.8 M

SHORTEST KEEPER
San Marino's Federico Valentini – **1.63 M**

1.5 M

Goalkeepers

The 'mad' member of the team, goalkeepers need a whole range of talents. It helps to be tall, but they also have to be good at both leaping high into the air and diving low on to the ground. They need quick reflexes, good positional sense and a strong pair of hands. They also have to be brave, throwing themselves at the feet of opposition strikers or jostling with them at corners.

The first goalkeeper gloves were made in the nineteenth century but most keepers still used their bare hands until well into the twentieth century.

1.2 M

€40.29
was the huge transfer fee for goalkeeper Gianluigi Buffon when he moved from Parma to Juventus in 2001, making him the world's most expensive keeper.

England's greatest-ever goalkeeper, Gordon Banks, was still experimenting with different types of gloves as late as the 1970 World Cup.

Modern gloves have a 'finger save' system that protects the goalkeeper's fingers from blistering shots and bullet-like free kicks.

0.9 M

0.6 M

0.3 M

Goalkeepers often have long careers. England's goalkeeper Peter Shilton played for **31 years**, and didn't retire until he was 47.

1990 1993 1999

Goalkeeper Peter Schmeichel from Denmark, won the Danish Player of the Year award three times.

The longest 'CLEAN SHEET' for a goalkeeper in international matches is held by Italian legend DINO ZOFF. He did not let in a single goal during a total **1,142** MINUTES of play.

31

Goalkeeper Nicky Salapu let in **31 goals** when his team American Samoa played Australia in a World Cup qualifier.

GOALKEEPERS OF THE CENTURY*

* As voted for by the IFFHS (International Federation of Football History & Statistics.

Gordon Banks
England
1963–1972

Lev Yashin
Soviet Union
1950–1970

Dino Zoff
Italy
1968–1983

Brazilian goalkeeper Rogério Ceni, did not just stop goals, he scored them. Lots of them! During the 2005 season, he scored 21 GOALS for São Paolo by taking their penalties and free kicks.

Head coaches

The head coach, or manager, is appointed by the club's owners to run the team. They decide which players to use, the tactics to adopt, and recommend players the club should buy to strengthen the team. The head coach of a national team selects the best players in the country to compete in big international tournaments.

Head coaches are as important as famous players for a team to be successful.

23

Many top players become **successful head coaches** like Barcelona's Luis Enrique. A few never played at all, such as Carlos Alberto Parreira, head coach of Brazil when they won the 1994 World Cup.

EUROPE'S MOST SUCCESSFUL HEAD COACHES

	Championships won					
	Champions League	Serie A	La Liga	Bundesliga	Premier League	Ligue 1
Pep Guardiola						
Barcelona	⚽⚽		⚽⚽⚽			
Bayern Munich				⚽⚽⚽		
José Mourinho						
Porto	⚽					
Chelsea					⚽⚽⚽	
Inter Milan	⚽	⚽⚽				
Real Madrid			⚽			
Carlo Ancelotti						
AC Milan	⚽⚽	⚽				
Chelsea					⚽	
Paris Saint-Germain						⚽
Real Madrid	⚽					
Luis Enrique						
Barcelona	⚽		⚽⚽			

FAMOUS HEAD COACHES

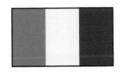

VITTORIO POZZO

Head coach of Italy in the **1930**s, and still the only international coach to lead a country to two World Cups.

SIR MATT BUSBY

The Scot led Manchester United to three league titles before his team was killed in an air crash, in **1958**. His rebuilt team won two more league titles, and Europe's top trophy.

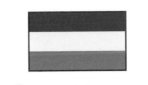

RINUS MICHELS

Turned Ajax Amsterdam into one of Europe's top teams in the 1960's, then took Netherlands to the final of the 1974 World Cup.

SIR ALEX FERGUSON

A Scottish manager who led Manchester United for 27 years! He won two Champions League titles and a record 13 Premier League titles.

Corinne Diacre is the **first female head coach** in the higher leagues of men's world football. She was appointed by French Ligue 2 side Clermont Foot in 2014.

Old Big Head was the nickname given to Brian Clough, one of football's most colourful head coaches. He took English team Nottingham Forest from the Second Division to the top of the First Division in just one year. Nottingham Forest then won the European Cup twice!

Huge pressure comes with the job of head coach. In top leagues, as many as HALF the head coaches are SACKED EACH SEASON.

Even **successful coaches are sacked,** like José Mourinho. He won the Premier League three times with Chelsea but was also dismissed twice by the club!

10:00

One of the **fastest sacking** in football history was Leroy Rosenior, just **10 minutes** after being appointed head coach by English club Torquay.

49

Penalty shoot-outs

One of the most thrilling and tense events in a football match is the penalty shoot-out. These are used in knock-out matches when there is no winner after full time and extra time. The teams take five penalties each, or more if necessary. Scoring the decisive penalty in a shoot-out is one of the greatest feelings in football. Missing it is the worst!

1970

The first English professional shoot-out was between Hull City and Manchester United, in 1970. It was won by Manchester United, 4–3.

LIVERPOOL have WON MORE PENALTY SHOOT-OUTS in knock-out tournaments than any other club in the English Premier League.

1977

First penalty shoot-out in the World Cup, when Tunisia beat Morocco, 4–2.

The first **World Cup** final to be decided by a shoot-out was the Italy vs Brazil final in 1994. Italy's Roberto Baggio had the misfortune to miss the decisive penalty, and Brazil won 3–2.

The most successful countries at World Cup shoot-outs:

Country	Shoot-outs		Won	Success rate
Germany	4	●●●●	4	100%
Argentina	5	●●●●●	4	80%
Brazil	4	●●●●	3	75%
France	4	●●●●	2	50%

LEAST SUCCESSFUL!

England is the worst country at World Cup shoot-outs, losing all three of the shoot-outs they have had to play.

Of the **240** penalties taken during WORLD CUP SHOOT-OUTS ...

69 MISSED

171 SCORED

The **2006 World Cup final** between Italy and France also went to a penalty shoot-out. Italy had learnt their lesson from their match with Brazil because they won this shoot-out 5–3.

48

PENALTY KICKS is the highest number ever in a shoot-out. This was at the end of the NAMIBIAN CUP FINAL in 2005. Fifteen of the penalties were missed but KK Palace eventually beat Civics 17–16.

Football fans

The fans are a key part of every football team's success. Players come and go, managers come and go, but fans remain loyal for life. Fans are the obsessive heart and soul of their team, whether it's their club or national side. Without fans, football would be far from the exciting show it has become.

Many **fans travel hundreds, or even thousands of miles** to watch their team play, not just within the country but abroad as well. Some clubs have so many travelling fans that they often easily outnumber the 'home' fans in the stadiums they visit.

Fans of **Red Star Belgrade** arguably create the most intense stadium atmosphere in the world, especially when they play their arch rivals Partizan of Belgrade. The electrifying atmosphere is partly to intimidate the opposition into playing badly!

Over **1** BILLION fans watch the World Cup tournament on television.

Football clubs know how important their fans are, and bigger ones keep them informed with club magazines, websites and even special TV channels.

FOOTBALL NEWS

Most countries have daily football newspapers, as well as football magazines to keep fans up to date.

Turkish football fans are the **loudest** in the world. Fans in Galatasaray's stadium can create a deafening noise of about 131 decibels! That's as loud as a thunder-storm!

Songs are part of football culture. Thousands of fans bellow out these anthems both before and during the match to inspire their team. Two of the world's most famous football songs are Liverpool's 'YOU'LL NEVER WALK ALONE' and Barcelona's 'BARCA CHANT'.

Many South American matches feature amazing firework displays. The most spectacular is the 'GREEN HELL' displays of Brazilian club Coritiba. The entire stadium, as well as sky, erupts with green fire and smoke.

Fans from different countries have different **favourite foods** to eat while they are watching football:

Argentina	SAUSAGE SANDWICH	
Bosnia and Herzegovina	SALTED GRAPES	
Germany	BRATWURST SAUSAGE	
Israel	SUNFLOWER SEEDS	
United Kingdom	MEAT PIES	

Referees

Although often criticised by fans, head coaches and the media for their decisions, referees are an essential part of football. They make sure that the match is played according to the Laws of the Game. Referees have lots of power: they can send off players, dismiss a manager from his dugout and even order a game to be abandoned!

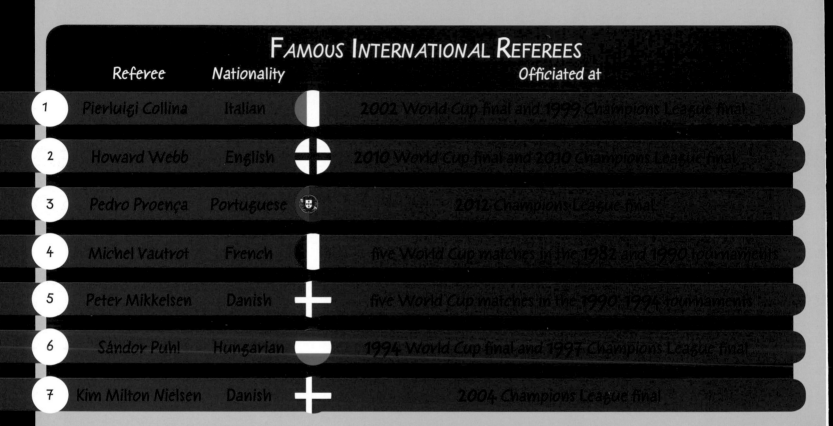

FAMOUS INTERNATIONAL REFEREES

	Referee	Nationality		Officiated at
1	Pierluigi Collina	Italian		2002 World Cup final and 1999 Champions League final
2	Howard Webb	English		2010 World Cup final and 2010 Champions League final
3	Pedro Proença	Portuguese		2012 Champions League final
4	Michel Vautrot	French		five World Cup matches in the 1982 and 1990 tournaments
5	Peter Mikkelsen	Danish		five World Cup matches in the 1990, 1994 tournaments
6	Sándor Puhl	Hungarian		1994 World Cup final and 1997 Champions League final
7	Kim Milton Nielsen	Danish		2004 Champions League final

Argentinian referee Damian Rubino holds the record for sending off the most players in a single match: all 22! He also red carded all the substitutes and both team coaches, handing out **36 RED CARDS** in total.

All referees carry **a whistle, a watch, penalty cards, a data wallet with pen and paper, and a coin** for deciding who gets the first kick-off in each half.

In football's early days, **referees weren't used as any disputes** were settled by a gentlemanly discussion and a shake of hands.

Referees use **HAND SIGNALS** to communicate what has happened on the pitch.

The badge on a referee's **left chest pocket** displays his licence, for example FIFA, English Premier League, La Liga, and the year it was issued.

GOAL

OBSTRUCTION

HANDBALL

PUSHING

Before the introduction of the whistle, referees indicated their decisions by waving a WHITE HANDKERCHIEF.

Oops! French referee Michel Vautrot is considered among the best ever, but in the 1990 World Cup semi-final between Italy and Argentina he forgot to check his watch. He allowed the first period of extra time to run to 23 minutes – it was meant to be only 15 minutes!

Sándor Puhl, another top international referee, failed to show even a yellow card to an Italian player who elbowed a Spanish midfielder and broke his nose, in the 1994 World Cup quarter-final between Italy and Spain. Italy won the match 2–1 and Spanish fans have blamed Puhl ever since.

Pierluigi Collini is thought of as the **best international referee of all time**. Immediately recognisable because of his bald head and 'staring eyes', he has officiated at both a World Cup final and a Champions League final, and was voted 'Best Referee of the Year' six years in a row.

Football in Asia

Televised World Cup and European matches have long been popular with Asian football fans, but it is only in recent years that many Asian countries have focused on developing professional football on home ground. Top Asian clubs like Chinese Super League team Guangzhou Evergrande have spent millions trying to make their team as successful as European clubs.

The **Asian Football Confederation**, or AFC, is the governing body of football in Asia, representing 47 countries ranging from Saudi Arabia and Syria in West Asia to China, Japan and Korea in East Asia, to India and Thailand in South Asia.

The **2022 WORLD CUP** will be held in QATAR, showing Asia's growing importance on the world football stage. **2002** was the only other time the World Cup took place in Asia, when it was jointly hosted by JAPAN and SOUTH KOREA.

Best performances in World Cups by Asian countries	Nation Reached Year	South Korea Semi-final 2002	North Korea Quarter-final 1966	Japan Last 16 2002	Saudi Arabia Last 16 1994

56

The **AFC Champions League** is the annual club competition in Asia, equivalent to the European Champions League. Two of the most successful teams in recent years have been South Korea's Pohang Steelers, who won in 1997, 1998 and 2009, and China's Guangzhou Evergrande who won in 2013 and 2015.

THE ASIAN CUP

is the most important national football competition in Asia. Held every FOUR YEARS, it is to decide Asia's best footballing nation.

South Korean striker **Ahn Jung-hwan** was sacked by Italian club Perugia after scoring the winning goal for South Korea in the second round of the 2002 World Cup against Italy. He was accused of 'ruining Italian football'!

JAPAN have won FOUR of the last SEVEN ASIAN CUPS.

Several Asian players have become big names in Europe, playing for top teams.

Shinji Kagawa
Japan

Club: Borussia Dortmund
Career high: Asian Cup winner

Shinji Okazaki
Japan

Club: Leicester City
Career high: English Premier League winner

Son Heung-Min
South Korea

Club: Tottenham Hotspur
Career high: Asian Cup runner-up

Park Joo-Ho
South Korea

Club: Borussia Dortmund
Career high: Swiss Super League winner

Brazilian player Alex Teixeira moved from Shakhtar Donetsk (Ukraine) to Jiangsu Suning (China) for £38 MILLION.

Brazilian player Oscar moved to Shanghai SIPG (China) for £60 million.

Rich Asian clubs have tried to boost their success by paying higher and higher transfer fees for top players.

Argentinian player Carlos Tevez moved to Shanghai Shenhua (China) for £52 million.

Brazilian player Ramires moved from Chelsea (England) to Jiangsu Suning (China) for £35 MILLION.

Business of football

Football today is BIG MONEY. At top clubs
transfer fees and players' and managers'
wages often run into many millions of pounds.
Today top players all expect to be
multi-millionaires and large
companies compete to pour
money into the game.

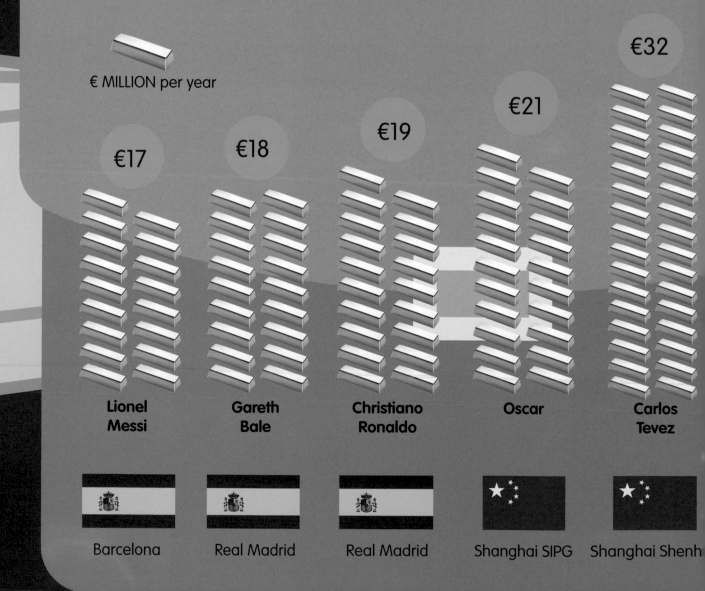

TOP FIVE HIGHEST-PAID PLAYERS

€ MILLION per year

€17	€18	€19	€21	€32
Lionel Messi	Gareth Bale	Christiano Ronaldo	Oscar	Carlos Tevez
Barcelona	Real Madrid	Real Madrid	Shanghai SIPG	Shanghai Shenh

£626 MILLION
The most expensive squad in world football is Manchester United.

Mega-rich Spanish club Real Madrid have repeatedly broken the **record for paying the highest transfer fee**. In 2000, they paid a record £37 million for Luis Figo, then in 2001 a record £46 million for Zinedine Zidane. In 2009, they broke the record again with £80 million for Cristiano Ronaldo, only to break it once more with an £85 million payment for Gareth Bale.

The most expensive TEENAGE footballers in history:

Anthony Martial	Luke Shaw	Lucas Moura
£36 million	£31 million	£28 million

FIERCE COMPETITION
The credit card company **Mastercard** had for many years 'partnered' the World Cup tournament, but they were pushed out by their rivals **VISA**.

The first English football tournament to be sponsored was in 1982, when the Milk Marketing Board sponsored the League Cup. Ever since, the tournament has been commonly referred to as the 'Milk Cup'.

TOP THREE FOOTBALL SPONSORS

The fast food giant MCDONALD'S has for many years sponsored football's two biggest international tournaments: the WORLD CUP and the EUROPEAN CHAMPIONSHIP. They also sponsor grassroots coaching of young players.

NIKE

Nike pays for players and teams around the world to wear their kits. In 2016, England, France, Portugal, Poland, Croatia, and Turkey wore Nike branded kits in the Euros, whilst Brazil and Chile wore them in the Copa América.

COCA-COLA has had stadium advertising at every World Cup since 1950. It has been an official World Cup partner since 1978.

Technology in football

Advanced technology plays a bigger and bigger role in football today. Electronic devices can show if the ball definitely crossed the goal line and can provide detailed statistics about the matches, allowing head coaches to analyse how to improve the team's performance.

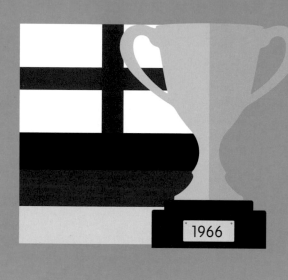

England's third goal in the 1966 World Cup final against Germany was **hotly contested** and even today, German fans still claim the ball never completely crossed the line.

1966

'Heat maps' show which part of the pitch each player has occupied the most. This sophisticated technology is a long way from the basics, such as how many corners and shots on goal have been taken!

108 STADIUMS around the world are authorised to use electronic systems known as **'GOAL-LINE TECHNOLOGY'** to confirm whether the ball fully crosses the goal line, or not.

HAWK-EYE is the most well-known of the goal-line technology systems, providing a series of CAMERAS TRACKING THE BALL. If the computer simulation shows that the ball has fully crossed the goal-line, this is immediately RELAYED to a special WATCH worn by THE REFEREE.

Opta is a **sports statistics** company, providing one analyst for each team. They record every single shot, header, pass, corner and save in a match and feed the data into a computer.

Many clubs are very protective about the **data collected** on their matches in case it helps the opposition!

CAIROS GOAL-LINE TECHNOLOGY SYSTEM works with a microchip inserted into the football. If the ball crosses the line, it triggers sensors under the grass.

The **Goalminder system** is a new form of goal-line technology. Readability cameras are built into the goal posts. This means that there is less chance of the ball running into a blind spot, where the camera can't see the ball.

Football on television

In the early days, professional football could only be seen if you squeezed through the turnstiles at the football ground. But since the sport has been televised, it has created bigger and bigger armchair audiences, totalling billions of people around the world.

The **first televised** match was in **1937** – a specially arranged fixture in **London**. The first **live** televised match in 1946 ended early because it became too **dark** and there were no **floodlights**.

Television has brought a **huge** amount of money into football, changing how **players** are viewed.

At first, clubs only allowed the **second half** of the match to be screened as they were concerned that showing the full match would **affect attendance**.

The English Premier League earns **over £2 BILLION** every year from televising matches.

BIGGEST TV AUDIENCES

International match
World Cup final

Club match
European Champion's League final

English League fixture
Manchester United vs Liverpool

Teams
First: Manchester United
Second: Real Madrid
Third: Barcelona

The English Premier League
Television matches are watched by up to 360 million viewers in Asia, making it the most popular foreign sort foreign sport on TV.

ADVANTAGES OF TV COVERAGE

Can increase attendance at matches as fans want to see the household names.

Keeps fans well-informed about their clubs.

Gives a close-up view of the action, with replays of key incidents.

The bigger audience helps football to attract wealthy sponsors.

VS

DISADVANTAGES OF TV COVERAGE

Cheaper viewing on television, can reduce match attendance.

TV and newspapers can sensationalise players' behaviour, giving football a bad name.

Fame can result in footballers losing their privacy.

TV coverage of football dominates the coverage of all other sports.

THE BIG SCREEN

Some cameras at football matches are there to make movies about the sport.

Recent Movies about Football:
Ginga: The Soul of Brazilian Football (2005)
The Damned United (2009)
Next Goal Wins (2014)

Index